Quite a few years ago, my Pastor, preached a sermon based on a character in one of Charles Dickens novels titled Great Expectations. This exceptional character was Miss Havisham. She had been jilted at the altar and, because of this, had become an angry and bitter woman. So bitter that she didn't remove her wedding dress or the wedding cake from the table for some time. How long? I won't pretend that I read the entire book to find out. From what I did read she is described as being very beautiful and rich once upon a time. That is, before she became bitter and sunlight became something she no longer welcomed. The topic of the

Pastors message was for us to not get stuck in our situations and past hurts. Learn to let things go and move on with life. Take that wedding dress off and get that molding cake off the table. Open the curtains and let in the sunshine.

Chapter 1

"Girl, don't you marry that man". My Godmother was trying her best to warn me. She had been my mothers' best friend until my mom died. " Those Johnsons are crazy as hell. Baby makers too. All of them tote them Bibles around but have no idea what those scriptures mean". Ma, I know his father is your cousin and all, but why are you judging Him? Just because the rest of the men in their family are crazy doesn't mean he is. Besides, I love him. Not only is he fine as hell with those perfectly straight teeth, those beautiful big brown eyes accented by those long eyelashes and perfectly placed dimples. But, on top of that, he's saved, sanctified and filled with the Holy Ghost! Not to mention that bangin' body! "Yeah, he filled with something, but the Holy Ghost aint't it. As soon as his baby mama find out about ya'll getting married she going straight to child support for an increase and you ain't never gone have no money. And heaven forbid your fast tail gets pregnant". Oh, come on Ma, you know I can't have any children. That's the one thing I wish I could give my mother before she dies. "Oh, Ruby is definitely is sure enough going to get that grandbaby before she passes away if you keep entertaining mister saved, sanctified, and filled with the Holy Ghost, Bible toting Howard Johnson. Trust me on that one. A hard head makes a soft ass Janine.

It all started out so innocently. After we moved in together, he was so protective of me; always waiting for me at the bus stop. I think I surprised him one day as I turned my key in the lock: "Janine, where the hell have you been? I've been back and forth to that bus stop twice! You know the routine. Call me when you're leaving your job so I can estimate what time you'll be getting on the subway. Call me after you get off the sub way so I can estimate what time you'll be getting on the bus so I can be waiting at the bus stop!" I thought this was so cute, but its really one of the first signs that he's an abuser. Control. Of course I explained to him that I'm not a clock and he has to ease back on that. I was going through enough. As if doing hair all day wasn't enough, but I was constantly being evaluated by the owners of the salon. They loved my work but were really focused on the fact that I didn't look the part. They frequently requested that I wear makeup and more stylish clothing. So, there I was, fighting two fights that I shouldn't be a part of. He was forcing me to look as unattractive as possible while my counterparts wanted the opposite. In those moments I sided with Howard because I thought he loved me so much that he didn't want anyone else looking my way. Control.

Marriage and two children later, we were finally able to afford a car. To ease the financial strain that a daycare bill would have put on us, I left the salon to become a stay at home mom. "Howard, can you take me to the store?" This was a stupid question coming from me because the answer was always 'no'. He stuck to his guns about wanting a *natural* woman. "Babeeeey, I found a car. It's a red 380zx". After a brief sigh I responded "isn't that a sports car? You do know that we have two children? And, what about the insurance? I know that insurance is higher on red cars and sports cars." "Everything is good. The insurance is straight and there are seats in the back. It's a good car." That night when he came home, I realized just how ignorant of a man Howard was. No seats in the back of the car. His testimony that night at Church took the cake as he talked about the goodness of God and the entire congregation came out to get a peep at our blessing. If I was light skinned I would have turned beet red as his father reminded him that he was a family man and needed to take that car back and get an appropriate

"We do offer a payment plan, Mrs. Johnson. There is a one hundred dollar deposit to get the divorce process started. If you wish to proceed, you can see the receptionist on your way out, sign the documents and pay your deposit". With that said, we shook hands and I headed out of his office and towards the receptionist desk. So simple. My Godmother had been right after all. Howard had proved to be crazier than a bed bug. After three children, one gorgeous girl and two overly handsome boys; moving from Maryland to North Carolina for a lower cost of living, my Knight in Shining Armor had abandoned us. He moved back to Maryland without even a simple goodbye. The only good that came out of the whole mess was our three children. Not to mention that my daughter had been born before my mother passed away. I had given her a grandchild. The marriage wasn't a good one. It was filled with emotional, sometimes physical abuse, little to know affection, and hate. I watched myself go from a beautiful and confident 20 year old woman with a million dreams and expectations to a 25 year old drained and hopeless one. "I'm going to take this over the road trucking job and the orientation is in

Maryland". I was beyond ecstatic because I had grown tired of borrowing money to pay the rent and standing in the line at the Salvation Army to pay the light bill. Well, that drop off to Greyhound Bus Station turned out to be the last I would see of my husband and father of my three children for at least two years. This trip to the divorce attorney had been a bitter one because, although I knew that I had done everything in my power to keep my marriage together. I had attended Church regularly, prayed all the prayers in a book titled "The Power of a Praying Wife", been anointed with the finest oil, taken care of my home, husband and children. After all that my final question to myself? How in the hell could my Minister husband walk out on his family while toting that Bible and being "saved, sanctified and filled with the Holy Ghost"? Back to my maiden name. Jackson, Miss Jackson if you're nasty.

Chapter 2

Hi, Nicky! What's going on in your neck of the woods? Nicky, or Nicole, had been my best friend since high school. Even though we never seemed to frequent the same state, we still remained close. She was the only person that I felt I could be completely honest with. About anything. Her husband was a military man and they had two children. A daughter in college and a son who was in high school. Even though we hadn't seen one another in four years. Distance couldn't keep us feeling as if we were in each others living rooms once we got on the phone. "Nothing much", Nicky answered. Same shit, different day. I laughed a quiet, sentimental laugh. "How was Church today", she asked. Oh, girl, It was the bomb. My Pastor preached about a character from one of Charles Dickens books called Great Expectations. "Are you talking about that old ass book from the eighteen hundreds?" Shut up and listen, I told her as I rolled my eyes. Anyway, she spoke about a character in a book called Great Expectations. Her name was Miss Havisham. What happened to her is that she got jilted at the altar and became so bitter that she didn't take her wedding dress off for a long time and even left the molding wedding cake on the table. Basically, she let her life get stuck in a rut out of bitterness and was never able to move on with her life. The topic of the sermon was for us to learn to forgive and move on with our lives. It was a great sermon but who does that? "You", Nicole stated bluntly". She didn't know it but I was standing in the middle of my bedroom with my head hung to the floor. I sighed. Not out of tiredness, but, because I knew she was right. I am nothing like that woman. "Oh, yes your ass is". Be honest with yourself Jay. When is the last time you had a man? And I'm not talking about those infrequent booty calls from Lucky". You see, I was still legally married to Lucky. We had been married for eleven years but only lived together for about three months. He was fine as hell with a nice, tight, young body. We were eleven years apart. I was thirty one when I married him so I'll leave the subtraction up to you. The sex was so good that I had set a three year abstinence goal when he was in jail. I'd waited patiently for those nice, long, deep strokes. That dude could eat pussy like he was getting paid in diamonds to do it. No one had ever been able to satisfy me like that. Getting fucked by him was like being transported to another world. All I could do was close my eyes because I didn't want to look at his fine ass or that tattoo of my name that emblazoned his neck. If I looked at him, the realization that he was a true piece of shit would mess up my orgasm. See, on the other side of pleasure, Lucky had wrecked cars, stolen money from me, and even managed to have three or more children that did not come from my womb. He never tried to be a good husband to me as he chose a life of constant incarcerations. After all his bullshit I could still fuck him like I didn't know he was a bastard. He could never come home again though. Fuck me, eat my pussy and get your ass out. He knew the rules. As I got caught up in my wetness I could hear the snapping of Nicole's fingers "earth to Janine". "Stop looking at them pictures of Lucky you got stored on your phone. You know you need to get rid of them divorce his young ass!" I laughed hysterically knowing she was absolutely right.

Lucky, Lucky, Lucky. (sigh). I don't even know how he got that nickname. I met him during a vulnerable point in my life. As a matter of fact, I sort of used him as a means to an end of another unhealthy relationship. Robert. " You look good in that outfit, girl". By this time I was about 18 or 19 and attending Beauty School in Fayetteville. My mother was stricken with kidney failure when I was a teen and we moved in with family. One of my classmates and I decided to hang out at the club. Back in those days, the IHOP, or International House of Pancakes, was the hangout spot after the club ended. "Who is he?', I thought as I eyed the good looking dude in front of me. He was medium height, light skinned with a denim outfit on that was covered with comic illustrations. Style too? Being the bold young woman I was: "Your outfit is nice. Where'd you get it?" "Thank you and I purchased it in Baltimore". Dang. He had dimples too. Before the night was over Robert was paying for my dinner and I was giving him my real name instead of Alexis, which was my fake one. I fell head over heels in love with him, but he was married. Go figure. When I was with Howard, oftentimes I would think about Robert and wish that he would have fathered my children. It wasn't so much that I really wanted him. It was more of the fact that I knew he would have been a great father. I was a witness to this in my younger years when I saw him with his own children. Years after our departure from one another, I ran into him again and we started our romance all over again. But, as fate would have it, he was living with his girlfriend and she was pregnant. While I enjoyed having regular sex and compliments daily, the fact remained that he was already involved and co habituating with another woman whom he was expecting a baby with. After reliving the words of Howard telling me how ugly I was, how fat I'd become, and his rants about how no other man would ever want me, I just didn't care anymore. Occasional love was better than no love. My self esteem was non-existent. So, that's what I settled for, an entire seven years of bullshit. So, I'll admit, when Lucky came into my life, I didn't exactly fight it. "The best way to get over an old love is to get a new one". A crock of shit. The devil is surely responsible because he gave me just what I wanted. Hell, let's be honest. The devil wasn't to blame for this one. My eyes and pussy were! That's the honest truth! I was 30 years old. Old enough to have common sense. "Sure, you can come over, my children just drifted off to sleep". It was a nice night and I'd been standing on my feet all day. Half of my day was spent at the hair salon and the other half was spent wiping asses and emptying bedside commodes at the homes of my home health clients. "Damn, I'm so sick of Robert and his selfish ass. My family this, my family that. Whining ass". Oh, how I wished I had a real companion to rub my feet and ask how my day was. Maybe Wal-Mart does carry EVERYTHING. This was the first time in seven years I wanted to entertain another man. I was so tired of Robert. "I'm coming", I yelled from the top of the steps in my apartment. Hello came out of my mouth with a deep breath that I hoped Lucky wouldn't notice. He was so handsome. Light-skinned, brown eyes, small frame, not too tall, not too short. Perfect. "Hi, beautiful" he said as I invited him in. After offering him something to drink and directing him to my living room couch, we made some small talk. He revealed that he was from the Washington, D.C area but had grown up in North Carolina. He was 25 years old, had a job, and was single. No drama. "You seem a little tense baby, he crooned. "Well, I'm okay. It's just that I haven't ENTERTAINED another man in a while so I'm just a little nervous". "Well, let's do something about that. When's the last time you had a good massage?" "Uhh, never". We both laughed and that cleared the air. The children's movie "The Incredibles" was already in the DVD player so I pushed play and relaxed so that I could enjoy my massage. And what do you know? He started by massaging my feet and asking how my day was!!! Oh, goodness. This was too good to be true! That turned out to be the best massage I've had in my 43 years of living. So different from what I had become accustomed to. Robert was good lover but he was selfish. It was always about him and his needs. We always made small talk and fucked. That was it. But Lucky was young and full of energy. That foot massage led to a back massage and him eating my pussy so good that I wanted to give him my bank card. Hahahaha. Eventually, I was forced to break things off with Robert for good and Lucky and I married. There's always a calm before the damn storm. I found out that Lucky wasn't 25. His ass was 20. He was hooked on cocaine, didn't have a driver's license, lost his job at Wal-Mart, and was a jail bird. We only lived together for about 2 months as the prison system became his home. When he wasn't locked up, he was busy making babies with at least 3 other women, and just being a total fuck up. Why does he call himself Lucky again?

Well, well, Ms. Jackson. The attorney shook my hands as I poised myself to fill out these divorce papers and give his receptionist another one hundred dollar deposit. Fortunately, this will be our last transaction, I jokingly said. A couple of months later when I opened the envelope, failure stained my face once again. A slow death. Somewhat akin to watching Barack Obama leave the White House and watching Donald Trump go in. I mean, we all knew that Barack had served his eight years but his departure still hurt like hell. This hadn't been my plan for my life. Forty three and twice divorced. But here I was, looking at another document with the heading "Dissolution of Marriage". Just like Miss Havisham I was done. Wedding dress still on and molding cake still on the table. Never would I allow love or any resemblance of it seep into my life.

<u>Chapter 3</u>

"Yes, Ms. Brown, You can come in Friday at 9'oclock". I had to be careful to record her appointment in my book as she was one of my older, loyal customers. Even though I was growing tired of these bi-weekly roller sets and French rolls, the bills still had to get paid. You could always depend on the older customers. They really just wanted a fresh, clean head of hair. I considered myself one of the best hairstylists in town. My skills varied from French rolls and press and curls to box braids and edgy hair cuts. But still, I was barely making it and in desperate need of a career change. With three grown children and a granddaughter, I should be living the best of my life. Something was missing. Money. Passion. Love. "Come on in Susan", I motioned to my next customer. She was an older lady who also happened to be an evangelist and a singer. "How are you doing baby?", she came in closer for her bi-weekly hug. "I'm doing fine Ms. Susan. How are you?" I asked as I made small talk and led her to the shampoo bowl. "I'm doing good" she answered. "I'll really be doing good after I move out of my house and leave my sorry ass husband". She didn't know it, but I almost sprayed water all over her face when she said those words. "What?!!!" "Yeah, girl, I'm tired. We are 70 years old and this negro still refuses to change. With me being an evangelist and a singer I can find another man. Honey, life is too short to put up with mess. I want somebody that wants me. Somebody that I can enjoy life with." As I gazed at her, I was uplifted by her confidence as a woman. Knowing that, at 70 years old, she was still confident enough in herself to not settle like so many women have. Not to just settle for anything as I had done so many times in my life. Wow! As Ms. Susan gathered her money to pay me, she looked at me and said: Don't settle for anything. If a man is not willing to give you what you need, there are plenty of Adam & Eve and other stores that have just what you need to please yourself". My astonishment at the bluntness of this woman made me want to holler all over the salon.

"Little girl, hold your head still!!" This is the shit I'm talking about!, I thought as I tried my best not to pop this child on the side of her head. All this for twenty five dollars? Taking that cape off and releasing her to her mother was the greatest joy in my life for the last two hours. As the were leaving all I could do was to shake my head as I really considered telling her momma to find that little brat another hairdresser. Silas, my co worker, came strolling into my private room, "What's on the menu today?" Nothing, as usual, for me. "I wish you would get you a man so you could have some business to tell". We both laughed. Look, I have already had two sorry ass husbands and the way my life has been going, I won't have another one. "Don't count yourself out so soon", Silas replied. Look, I'm already forty three. Most of the men out here are just damn crazy. The older ones are already set in their ways looking for a young girl to cook and clean for their old, dusty asses. The younger ones are looking for a momma and I'm tired of raising kids. I'm not into older men anyway. An old ass man depending on me to arrange the medicine in his pill case doesn't sound too exciting. And, I'm not helping him get ready to fuck by using any kind of apparatus. Silas almost fell out of his chair. Did you see the meme on Facebook that says the younger men come with a big dick, nice, fat tongue ready for action. But, their asses also come with no job, a weed habit that they expect you to pay for, and a playstation. I just can't! Denean, one of the other hairstylists, must have heard our loud asses as she came sauntering down the hallway. "While ya'll down here laughing did you see the new label on the thermostat? Silas and I unanimously said "what sign"? Denean laughed and said "the one that says to leave the thermostat on seventy degrees". Shiittt! Does she know how cold it is in this salon? The gossip fest was on now as we talked about the salon owner of N'Sync Hair Salon. While she was very nice and a talented stylist, she had begun to neglect her duties as an owner. Sometimes not showing up for appointments or returning customers phone calls. Not to mention her new beau who made everyone in the salon uncomfortable. She had put him in charge as the salon manager. Often, he flitted about like he was on speed or something. He didn't actually DO anything. He just walked around so fast that it looked as if he was doing something. Since his presence, we all had been accused of everything from stealing the booth rent from the locked and secured box to being racially offensive to a customer who came in for an eyebrow wax. The reasons the three of us stayed is because it was a beautiful salon and the booth rent was the most reasonable in town. Well, I will see the two of you later, I remarked as I tidied up my room. "Ok, Denean said as Silas gave me the side eye.

Chapter 4

"Why is my stomach rumbling, I asked myself as I headed toward Owen Drive. I hadn't eaten all day! Making a left onto Owen drive I headed toward highway 301 and turned into the Waffle House parking lot. "Can I start you out with something to drink Maam?" Coffee and ice water with extra ice, please. "Will that be regular or decaf?" Regular. As I waited patiently for my drinks and ultimately my food, I tried to brush off the dirt of the day. Gathering my things after paying my bill, Mister walked in. Yes, I'm calling him Mister from here on out. My body began to shudder immediately and I'm so happy that nobody would be able to notice the perk of my nipples. What in the hell is wrong with me, I reasoned with myself as I tried to stabilize my wobbly knees. I don't like dark skinned me. He was bald. I don't like bald men. Having this brief conversation in my mind he interrupted me by asking if he knew me from somewhere. Maybe from his wife, he uttered. That word me as I denied my familiarity, closed the door to Waffle House and got into my car.

Chapter 5

"Where are you going momma",my daughter asked as I headed out to the newly built Wal-Mart. I'm going to the store to get the ingredients for this casserole I saw on Facebook. Fifteen minutes later as I browsed the aisles I was met with a familiar looking face. Oh hell no! Not Mister. "We keep meeting up like this" he said. His voice and the fact that he had on a work uniform was enough to make me stand still like I was in formation. But his last words from three weeks ago haunted me. Wife. "I found out why your face was so familiar to me. We are friends on Facebook and I see your recipe posts all the time." Wow, I said numbly. That explains it. Other customers maneuvered their carts around us as we talked for at least an hour and he revealed that he was separated from his wife and that they were living apart. The more he talked the wetter I got. His voice was like Ving Rhames in Baby Boy. The fact that I hadn't had a man to even touch me in over a year may have had something to do with it, but, I swear, I could have fucked him right there. Right in the aisle of that Wal-Mart on Highway 301.

Olive Garden is always a great place for a first date. Food and laughter. The conversation was better than the food as Mister and I talked about everything from politics and education to celebrities and Jeopardy. Ending the night at a hotel was nice too. My plans were to keep my legs closed as tight as possible but when he smoothly asked "Can I have you tonight?" My pussy said yes before my mouth even opened. I mean, I don't fancy myself as being a hoe, but, I may have a few hoe tendencies which I'm proud to say I don't give into very often. "Excuse me", I asked, in total shock and awe. It was like a scene in a movie. I was Halle Berry and he was fine as Omari Hardwick from Power. Grappling with my decision wasn't really a struggle. Hell, I hadn't been touched in a year. The last man I dated had diabetes, high blood pressure, sleep apnea, back problems AND erectile dysfunction. Having sex with him was so-so and I was as scared as a virgin whose parents were at Bible Study while she was at home trying to get her first lay. All in all, it turned out to be a good night as we drifted off to sleep in that Skibo Road hotel.

      The following morning I didn't know whether I felt like a hoe or the beautiful woman Mister made me feel like I was as I tiptoed into my house that Saturday morning. Haha. Let me stop lying. I felt like a beautiful woman. It felt sooo good. Even though the actual sex wasn't that great it was the intimacy I craved. The touching and kissing. The sounds coming from his mouth as he moaned in pleasure. The look on his face as my wetness seemed to permeate through the condom and make him scream as he came. I loved that shit.

IS IT BAD THAT I NEVER MADE LOVE

NO, I NEVER DID IT

BUT I SURE KNOW HOW TO FUCK

I'LL BE YOUR BAD GIRL

I'LL PROVE IT TO YOU

I CAN'T PROMISE THAT I'LL BE GOOD TO YOU

CAUSE I'VE HAD SOME ISSUES

I WON'T COMMIT

NOT HAPPENING

Wale was the man. I always loved this song and wanted these lyrics to mirror me; but I had made love and I really wasn't a bad girl. I wanted to commit. But, deep down inside I knew that all men were just small pieces of shit.

Chapter 6

"Ma, you sure have been spending a lot of time with that man", my daughter Ciara said. Yeah, and what about it? I immediately jumped to the offensive because ever since I started dating him my children had begun to treat me differently. I believe they had a hard time knowing that I was doing the same things in the bedroom that they were doing with their significant others. To add to that, they had gotten comfortable with me being there for their every beck and call to babysit and be their taxi. Especially my daughter. While I loved each one of my three children and my granddaughter, the truth was I longed for an adult life with adult conversations and ideals. When I was married to their father I was a stay at home mom and after he left I fashioned my entire life around them and their needs. They were gown now and change was needed in my life. Mister provided that. We could talk about anything; from politics to pop culture. "Well, I'm just saying Ma, I don't like him". And what reason could you possibly have for not liking him when you don't even know him!! "He just has that LOOK". What look, Ciara? "That PLAYER LOOK. You know what I'm saying, Ma. He LOOKS like he has a girlfriend in every city he goes to. Those black lips LOOKING like he smokes weed. You KNOW the LOOK". My daughter, Ciara was the oldest of my three children and super protective of me. At 21 years old she was the most beautiful woman I've ever seen. She was married with a 2 year old daughter and had a successful career as a nail technician. I had raised her to be smart and independent. I had to admit that she was an excellent judge of character. Five years ago, I got into a relationship with a janitor at the high school she attended. Lucky, my second husband had moved to Virginia and after a year of no contact with him I decided to move on. Mr. Baker was nice with a J.O.B. and his own place. It didn't matter to me that he was a janitor. He was a nice guy, and , at first sight, his only flaw was that he didn't have a car. Oh, he had a car but it was in the shop being fixed. Same tired ass car story as every other man. Two months of joy and then the bullshit came. "Jay, I really have feelings for you and I hate to have to tell you this, but... I'm going to have to move back to California with my mom". I was a little taken aback because, although I knew he had some things to work out (like getting that mysterious car out of the shop), moving to California had never been one of our conversations. What are you talking about Baker/ You have your own place, a job, and a daughter who's right here in Fayetteville. What's really going on? " The owner of the building I live in is selling and all tenants have to be out by the first of January. This caught me completely off guard and I wasn't financially prepared so I'm stuck between a rock and a hard place". After taking two to three deep breaths, "You can stay with me". Look, I said, I can help you and you can help me. We are already a couple; your job is within walking distance from the house and you can help out with the bills. This seemed to be such a great idea at the time but, honestly, I must have lost my mind. Mr. Baker turned into a spineless, punk ass, pimply butt having, cry baby who expected me to be his transportation, uniform presser, cook, and sex goddess. He wanted all this while never giving me one penny. Every time I asked him for money he would break out in tears. Real fucking tears. On top of that, he asked me to have his baby!!! To keep that poor ass of a dream from coming true, I put on a sanitary pad every day for 30 days and told him I was bleeding so bad that I needed to see a doctor. There was no way in hell he would ever get this coochie again. Best acting job of my entire life. "Do you even want to know why I'm leaving ?" (he asked after my 30 day stunt). You aren't fulfilling my sexual needs". I was so relieved when he moved out. I silently clapped for myself and those sanitary pads when I saw him carrying bags of grocery in the rain a couple of weeks ago. The recounting of that story about Mr. Baker goes back to the fact that my daughter was then and is still now an excellent judge of character. She told me then not to date Mr. Baker because he was very childish and would never be mature enough for me. But I felt differently now. "Look, baby, I totally understand what you're saying but this different. You're not in my situation. You are still young and beautiful with a perfect body to match, and you have a husband. I haven't dated in years. Body not so perfect and time is passing me by. Why should I continue to sit in my room and grow old if there's a chance to do something else? If I get hurt, then I'll deal with it". But, Ma, you too, are still young and beautiful! You don't have to settle for some player! And he's married! He'll never give you the love and respect you deserve. All he's going to do is use you and throw you away like a piece of trash! "Ciara, I'm grown! I've given you and your brothers my whole life! Let me live!! I love you, Ma, and I don't mean to be disrespectful. With tears streaming down my face, we hugged. "I'll be okay, baby. I promise".

Chapter 7

What's going on with you?" Silas and Denean nosed their way into my business as usual. "We see that pep in your step" Denean teased. So, being me, I let them in on the tea. I was the happiest I'd been in a long time. Even Nicole noticed the change in my voice when we spoke and she was miles away. "Don't think I haven't noticed that you haven't been calling me as much. I've been preoccupied with the rigamaroll of getting used to working in this new dialysis center but I'm not that preoccupied. Fess up." Being backed into a corner I gave it up reluctantly. Nicole was my friend and I already knew that once she heard that he was married all the great things I had to say about him would fall on deaf ears. "Look, I know you're saying that this man is all that and a bag of chips, but you have to be careful. I don't want you to turn into that Miss Havisham lady but I also don't want to see you get hurt. Just watch yourself".

    The next few months were wonderful. I was actually dating at 43 years old. We began to get extremely close through our daily outings and 3 to 4 hour conversations every night. Real conversations. Not about sex or stupid stuff. Real, mature conversations. I don't remember ever having this kind of relationship. The sudden ringing of my phone followed by his sultry voice was music to my ears. "Hi handsome." "Hello beautiful". Then an uncomfortable pause: "We need to talk". In a five minute span of time, all of my hopes and dreams had been shattered. When Mister and I started seeing each other he had expressed an interest in moving to Georgia. What he failed to tell me is that he

AND his wife were moving to Georgia. While I understood his desire to leave little broken down Fayetteville, I never thought he would just cast me away. I had done something that I hadn't let myself do in almost twelve years. Hope. See, with two divorces under my belt, I had completely given up on that part of my life. It just seemed that no matter what I did, how beautiful or smart I was, men never thought I was good enough for them. Knowing this, I adjusted my life so I wouldn't harp on those things. My three areas were work, home, and Church. My vices were simple: television and coffee. Through all of my painful experiences, I had come to accept that love just wasn't for me. When I met Mister, I allowed myself to hope again. " Look Janine, you know that I care about you, but you knew from the start that I was married. I never lied to you about anything and you had a choice". What the fuck are you talking about? You told me that you were married but separated and that you had no intentions of reconciling with her; that she had cancer but had put you through so much that you just didn't want to be with her. "I don't remember saying that". Yeah, how quickly we forget the lies we tell. I was so disgusted! " So please tell me, what was all of this about? Why would you bring me into your life when you knew exactly what you had planned? Why me?! After I told you about all the bullshit that I've already been through? I screamed at him through the phone as I was only met my silence and sounds that I know too well: the silence of a man who doesn't give a fuck.

    The month following my latest catastrophe was harder than I ever thought it would be. I became depressed, couldn't eat and started to lose weight. Every love song on the radio made me cry. Sometimes being at work was too hard for me. Each time the entrance bell sounded at the salon I was met with knowing it wasn't him coming through the door. I just wanted to disappear into the night never to be seen again because being in a world without him just seemed pointless. "Janine, you better get yourself together", flowed from the mouth of my customer Cindy. Never let any man steal your joy; nor a woman either. It'll get better. Always, no matter what you're going through, get up, get dressed and go. If you continue to do this to yourself the only person hurting is you. He got what he wanted. Fuck him and the horse and carriage you THOUGHT he rolled in on". Ms. Cindy was crazy but I knew she was dead right. From that day, I gathered up my courage and took control of myself. Let me put in this last hairpin and you'll be ready to go Cindy. "I think your phone is ringing Jay; there's a man's face on it". Hello? "Hi Janine, I need to see you". Mistake.

"Things didn't go as planned with the move and I have filed divorce papers. Right now I'm in the process of renting a house because I've decided to stay in this area. The bottom line is that I want you to move in with me". I couldn't believe my ears. For once in my life, things were looking up for me. Yassss!!!

Chapter 8

"Janine, are you out of your mind?" Nicole's advice echoed in my ears. "What about his wife? What if one day he decides he wants her? Again. He's going to leave your lovestruck ass right back at square one". Nicky and my co workers at the salon had given me more advice than I could take. At the end of the day I'm a grown ass woman and can take care of myself. I loved him. I wanted him. " Even though my children are grown they are not responsible enough to totally live on their own. And this way, if we ever need a break from each other I'll have somewhere to go. We agreed with a long tongue filled kiss and my key". The next few months were as blissful as the first. Going to sleep with him and waking up to him was wonderful; not that we didn't have our moments but the good outweighed the bad. In my heart, I longed for him to be my husband. When I was with him I felt loved and wanted. I would go to work every day, go home to check on my children, go back to Misters house and take care of his two dogs and make sure his 18 year old son was okay. I handled the bills for him and he handled me when he wasn't working. I was in heaven in this beautiful house, a beautiful deck to sit on while drinking my coffee. I felt so in tune with myself as a grown woman. Not just a mother, a grandmother or hairstylist, but a beautiful woman that my man couldn't wait to get home to. This was the life I wanted. Then, in he came. Sexy and chocolate. I couldn't wait to have him. Walking around the bedroom with his towel tightly knotted around his waist while drying off his sexy, bald head with another, he interrupted my thoughts "What do you say we go out to dinner tonight because we need to talk". Not more bullshit! I screamed inside of myself. Every time he said those four words it was never good.

The sight of blood seeping out of his steak was enough to turn my stomach. Chicken critters was enough for me along with a loaded sweet potato. "Babe, I know that we've grown closer over these couple of months and we've been spending a lot of time together. Don't get me wrong. I'm enjoying myself but truth be told I'm tired of truck driving and I want to do something different with my life. I never really changed my mind about moving to Georgia. It's just that things didn't work out the way I planned. What I'm saying is that I'm still going to move to Georgia in the Spring after my son finishes this semester at Fayetteville Tech". And there I was. Speechless.

"Please tell me that you're going to leave his black ass alone!" Denean was crowding my space but she was right and I knew it. "Jay, come on! Do you need to be slapped in the motherfucking face to realize he's just been playing you? First, he tells you that his wife has cancer. Terminal cancer. Well, hell, it looks like she's still alive to me! I know it seems harsh but it's true!" I knew she was only speaking out of love and concern but, still, I couldn't walk away. Mistake

<u>Chapter 9</u>

No Church for me today. That meant no hour long ride to Ellerbee. We didn't have Church on the third and fifth Sundays. "Good morning sleepy head, Misters soothing voice filled my mind with all kinds of sinful thoughts. As I reached for his swollen dick, he pulled my hand away. "Be good baby, it's Sunday. Here's your coffee and breakfast is waiting on you downstairs". Maybe I was dreaming last night, I reasoned with myself but knew how wrong I was. Moments like this made me want to block out his words from last night. Reality as well as a whiff of my morning breath made me sit up as I sipped on this steaming cup of Caramel Starbucks coffee skillfully put together by the man I wanted so desperately to love me. Family time, movies, music, and great food filled the house on Sundays. Everything seemed normal. At the end of Sunday excitement, I turned in early with a steamy tub of bubbles waiting for me. At this house there was Mister, his brother Tony, his son John, and one of his workers on the truck named Justin. A house full of men smoking, cursing and eating. But I never minded and was always made comfortable. It was quite different at my house. Not that my house was bad, I just had more to do there. As I stepped out of my bath and wrapped the towel around me I could hear footsteps nearing the bedroom door. "I know you didn't think that I was going to leave you alone for too long", Mister said as he slowly closed the bedroom door. My body immediately went limp as he boldly approached me and drew my face to his in a passionate kiss. That kiss made me moan as if he were inside of me already. I had been watching him all day. Those grey sweatpants paired with a size "smedium" shirt accenting his bulging biceps. Lust had been my friend all day as I watched him cooking. The way he manhandled me in bed set my body on fire. Stroking me gently with just a hint of roughness from behind, he moaned "I've been wanting to fuck you all day". Why didn't you. I've been watching you all day too? With roughness in his voice as he was about to come he moaned "I had to fry that damned chicken."

"How are things going?" Nicole was on a fishing expedition of my life. It's been good. He hasn't said anything else about moving so I hope he's changed his mind. "Jay, you are always on a hoping, wishing, praying mission with that dude". We laughed a hearty laugh. I am in no way offended by her jokes because I know the truth but just don't want to accept it. I'm in love, I reply. "Whose love, Jay?" What you are doing is compromising yourself for some affection, attention, and some dick!" Yes, I laughed. And some cream colored carpet! We both hollered into the phone.

Chapter 10

Mary Bill's is a nice little café off Bragg Boulevard. It had become our meeting spot for my co workers and I to unwind and talk business. Our discussions consisted of talking about cosmetology classes, products, and advertising plans. I appreciated my co workers because no matter what we talked about, their ideas were always great. "Alright ya'll. What kinds of specials are we going to run this month to bring some business into this raggedy ass salon?" Silas was a trip> Not gay. Just a trip. I spit coffee everywhere and people watched as they secretly wanted in on our conversation. Time well spent.

All that time discussing our ideas and I had let time slip away from me as I remembered that Mister would be home in a couple of hours. He had been gone since Tuesday and Friday had snuck up on me. Opening the front door, Bella's smell hit me like a ton of bricks. She was in a cage in the kitchen that she had filled with piss and shit. After I put her out and began to clean her cage my cell phone rang as his face lit it up and I smiled. "Hi babe. What took you so long to answer the phone?" I was cleaning Bella's mess. "I need to talk to you". The dreaded words. "Look, I'm not going to have a lot of time to spend with you this weekend so I need you to go home for a couple of days. My wife is coming." My head started to spin as I tried to absorb his words without losing my mind. What in the hell did he just say to me? I, Janine, who had become his personal maid, errand runner, dog shit cleaner, and dick worshipper was going to have to gather my shit and go back home to my family like a puppy with its tail tucked between its legs to make room for another woman? All of this time while I constantly wrestled with thoughts in my mind about me just being something temporary to him and having him to tell me that I was wrong and paranoid. That phone call proved that I hadn't been crazy or paranoid after all. A few days after being "demoted" Mister called to let me know that though he cared for me he did not love me and was never nor could ever be in love with me. He very bluntly reminded me that I should have known what I was getting into and stated how devoted he was to his wife. My heart almost burst as he confessed that I was just something to do and his permanency in my life had only been a figment of my imagination. In the midst of the first phone call, I did the only thing I could do. I packed my bags, removed his key from my key chain and gave it to his son, and I left.

Chapter 11

    This breakup lasted about a month before Mister lured me back into his web of bull shit. He was a great cook and he knew just what to do and say to catch me. "Look, I apologize for what I said last time and about how I have treated you in the past. The truth is that I love you and I want to be with you. You bring out the best in me. The house even feels different when you're there. I know that I'm an asshole sometimes but, I've been trying to keep you arms length because I don't how to handle my feelings for you. Everything I said about not caring for you was a lie". Now, I'm not a glutton for punishment but Mister had a hold on me that I just could not shake. My key was given back to me and we returned to our normal arrangement. Almost. Even though I still loved him I became more reserved and made sure that I was not at his every beck and call. I tried to play "the game". Hell, who was I trying to fool? I didn't even know the name of the game or the directions. "Girl, you need to put his ass on ice. Make him want you and stop being so loving and available. Fuck that shit. You know that you are the bomb.com and you shouldn't be putting up with nobody's bullshit". My customer, Lisa was as raw as they come. She was straight up and from Brooklyn, New York. "You are crazy, Lisa. I just want to know why do I have to play a game anyway. Why can't it be simple? I'm so tired of this. I just want to be happy. Damnit!" Yeah, I know what you're saying but it's just not that easy. The way you're talking is like ole' boy is staying with his wife out of guilt, but cancer or no cancer, if you don't want to be with somebody, then you don't. You can still support them but there's a way to do things. You can't keep letting him push you to side every time she wants to come "home". You are not a pair of mobile steps. "I know and I'm hoping that this time will be different". I hope so for his sake. You know I can gather some homeboys from up the way to beat his ass. " Girl, shut up". I laughed so much at the thought of someone beating him up.

Chapter 12

I was back in my comfort zone. Full run of the house. Walking on my cream colored carpet while waiting for the love of my life to get home every night. Being taken out to eat every night. We had grown so close. "Hey, baby. I'm taking these pork chops out for dinner tonight. Is there anything in particular you want to go with it?" No, sweetie; whatever you fix is fine. You know I'm not picky. Then, the shit hit the fan. "Excuse me, baby; I have to take this phone call". I already knew that tone in his voice. It was Princess. That was my name for her anyway. " Jay?" I waved my hand in the air as I picked up my Michael Kors purse and the keys to my 2006 Buick Rendezvous. "But, Bae, let me explain. My stepson got arrested and we have to get the car from the impound and my stepdaughter's birthday is today so they are driving up". I took one step toward the door and with my heart racing, I turned back around and took a deep breath and let his black, 5'7" , bald headed, narcissistic ass have it. "I am so so motherfucking tired of you and this bullshit ass, fake ass marriage of yours.

One day you're in love with me and we are the couple of the year. As soon as that bitch calls you push me to the side like I'm just one of your fuck buddies! So what are you going to do now, move her ass in? Because I know that conversation was about more than getting a car out of the impound and your stepdaughters birthday! With that, he turned his back to me and put his head down. "What the fuck?" Are you serious? After all that I have done? Why would you fuck me over like this? For that hoe? Yeah, I did some research on Princess. I know all about her criminal history, her bunch of fucking kids, million marriages and her drug history. That bitch probably doesn't even have cancer. And now you're talking about celebrating her daughters birthday? The same one who didn't call for your birthday or Christmas? "Jay, stop! You don't know shit! He screamed at me from the top of his lungs". Yes I do know. I know she ain't nothing but a motherfucking hoe that uses you for your money. I know that's why you're paying twelve hundred dollars a month for this house and why you bought that new Jaguar!! All for some lazy ass hoe that could give two fucks about you! Who's here when you come from work tired and hurting? Who is there for you when you're stressed out and you need to talk for three or four hours? Who has been taking care of your house and your goddamned dogs while you're out buying Jaguars and I'm driving a car with over 200,000 miles on it? Who is fucking you and sucking your dick every day?? With tears coming down my face and almost out of breath, "Me. Me motherfucker. While you constantly look past me and brush me off for that bitch and whomever else you're fucking. He never turned around; just stood there with his back to me staring at the ground. "I gave you way too many chances. I should have left your bitch ass in Wal-Mart". I flung that worthless ass key to the ground, became friends again with Michael Kors and slammed the door. Walked out like a boss and got into my Buick Rendezvous with its over 200,000 miles and power steering leak and drove slowly away from the man I loved, the house I loved with the cream colored carpet I loved and the Jaguar outside that should have been mine.

There I was. Almost a year after I let my guard down and allowed myself to give into the man at the Waffle House on Highway 301. Then again at the Wal-Mart on 301. Standing in front of my house in Hope Mills. The house filled with people that I helped to create. Furniture I had purchased. Food I had supplied. All this and I didn't want to go in. Why? Because I didn't want to talk or answer questions on what happened. My granddaughter calling his name every time my phone rings because she automatically assumes that every time it rings it's him. I wanted to go back to my house. The one with the dogs and cream colored carpet. I had let myself get comfortable.

HURTS ME THE MOST WHEN I WAKE

I FUMBLE AND TWIST

TILL THE TRUTH STARTS TO CLICK

THERE'S SO MUCH SPACE IN THIS BED

THESE SHEETS GO FOR MILES

DREAMS OF YOUR SMILE

I DON'T WANT TO BE JUST A MEMORY

AND I DON'T WANNA FEEL

YOUR WINGS BREAK FREE

CAUSE WITHOUT YOU I'M LOST IN THE BREEZE

I GOTTA BE STRONG NOW

I GOTTA SHOW YOU HOW

I LOVE YOU LIKE I'VE NEVER EVER LOVED SOMEBODY

I'LL GIVE YOU THINGS YOU DIDN'T EVEN KNOW YOU WANTED

DON'T TELL ME THAT IT'S NOT ENOUGH

MY TIME IS UP

YOU'RE OVER US

CAUSE I THINK I MIGHT DO

ANYTHING FOR YOU

IF YOU JUST LET ME

IF YOU JUST LET ME

IF YOU JUST LET ME

JUST LET ME

TASTE OF YOUR LIPS IS STILL FRESH

THE SMELL OF YOUR SCENT

HOW COULD I FORGET

YOUR WORDS...HOW THEY CUT ME TO SHREDS

BUT TO TELL YOU THE TRUTH, EVERY PIECE IS FOR YOU

(Sinead Harnett featuring Grades. If you let me)

"Are you shitting me, Janine", asked Nicole. I wish I was but that's what happened. I'll tell you right now...it won't happen again. This dating and relationship shit is not for me. Tyrese was on Wendy Williams' show yesterday and he said he's off the market. Michael Eely is married. I'm going to call Trey Songz manager and ask if he's available for a fuck and a movie once a month, I joked. "I can't believe you're taking this so well, Nicole said. By the sound of her voice she was contemplating on temporarily committing me to the psych ward of Cape Fear Valley Hospital. "Janine, remember when we were talking about that lady in the book your Pastor preached about?" Yeah, Miss Havisham. "Don't become her. I joke a lot about you becoming like her but don't let this asshole turn you into her. He was fucked up and karma is real. There is a good man out there who is going to love you like you deserve". I hear you Nicky, but I don't think I'll ever be ready. Maybe with time. A lot of time. My doctor told me to stay away from any kind of stress because my blood pressure was slightly elevated at my appointment the other day. My plan is to stay away from all bastards, I mean men, and to relax. We laughed until our stomachs hurt.

Chapter 13

Speeding down Legion road trying to make it to the salon before my ten o'clock customer got there was interrupted by a text saying that she was going to be thirty minutes late. Yes! Now I can stop at McDonalds for a steak bagel combo with a coffee and orange juice. "Welcome to McDonalds, can I help you?" Yes, I'll have the steak bagel combo with a coffee and an orange juice. "Okay, your total is seven dollars and seventeen cents". I always thought 717 was my luck number because it was my building address where I grew up in Washington, D.C on Brandywine street. As I approached the payment window, my reminiscing was interrupted by my ringing cell phone. Hello? "Yes, this is Nurse Ratchett calling from Cumberland Medical and I'm calling to speak with Janine Jackson". Yes, this is Miss Jackson. "We need for you to come back in as soon as possible". For what? I'm on my way to work. "Well, Miss Jackson , we don't usually do this over the phone, but, your urine sample that was collected during your exam has confirmed that you are pregnant". Tears streamed down my faced as I handed the seven dollars and seventeen cents to the cashier. In the words of my former lover....no more shitting on the curb while telling everyone the dog did it.

Made in the USA
Middletown, DE
25 February 2024